THIS *Little* BOY

THIS *Little* BOY

BRANDON ALLEN

World Stage Press
Verse from the Village

BRANDON ALLEN

World Stage Press
Verse from the Village

BRANDON ALLEN

This Little Boy
© 2022 Brandon Allen
ISBN: 978-1-952952-31-9

Second Edition, 2022

Printed in the United States of America

Illustrations by Eanaj Janae / merakidynasty.com
Cover & Layout Design by Emily Anne Evans

This book is dedicated to my most gorgeous daughter, SYNAI JOY ALLEN. This is the first of what's to come and I am more than proud of you! You have shown me that regardless of what comes your way, with God's grace it can be molded into something beautiful and full of purpose. You are my legacy and I refuse to leave you undone!

Contents

THIS *Little* BOY

The Boy

Born and raised in the southern burbs
Where a mother nursed a father's hurt
She took his hand
Married the man
And there this little boy was birthed

It started off a fairy tale
But heaven quickly felt like hell
Traumas Noose
Substance abuse
Made home feel more like a jail

A boy caught in depression's web
The lies constantly filled his head
Pains well grew deep
Would torment his sleep
And these poems are the tears he shed

BIRTH OF ABUSE

I looked in her eyes and she could barely be recognized

Eyes glazed over and made me wonder if this is what it would look like if the moon cried

I cried 'cause I had never seen her this lifeless.

All that time spent making up herself it seems there were still spots she missed;

Like for example:

There's no concealer to cover up the residue left from her being abused...

Times when she was forced to lock lips glossed with material things to substitute for the pain he brings...

Fist - swell lips - so, he gave her two shots of collagen...

Or even when she fills herself up with as many capable suitors as she possibly can -

Then allow them to scrape out the remains of another just to make room for more since

This parent didn't properly plan!

And since her mirror never reflected an acceptable image she took - matters into her own hands

Pills down her own throat

And knife to her own wrists

Plus other parts she didn't want to exist...

They -

Pumped stomach...

Stopped bleeding...

Placed stitches and IVs in...

Just so she could finally get to see

the plastic surgeon.

THIS LITTLE BOY

I remember my first real poem: I sat at the computer while my tears stroked the keyboard the pain unlayered within the stanzas and my anger lashed out in metaphors. I repeated *Why?* from line to line questioning character and purpose to God's design.

This one individual couldn't belong to him. I thought - this one distributor of sorrows and agony could not be cut from the same cloth as me. I mean, how did I arrive from those loins and couldn't he see that my blood shed didn't match that which he came to be... and this was my reality. And it didn't belong in your picture-perfect TV sitcom.

See, I lived in a *'Different World'* where my *'Family Matters'* didn't belong. My life was unfamiliar and these *'Different Strokes'* would wither away at my *'Good Times.'* And I had no idea where I fit in.

I had a skewed image of what a black man is supposed to look like. In fact, I didn't even like how I looked, so the image of anything was better than this!

See, this is a story of an unidentified human project that was molded into something that nobody could recognize. It became a reflection of what was popular at the moment and always dressed in his best self-consciousness. Wrapped in how many different shades of *fake* his facade could portray...

And no one took notice.

No eyes cut to his cuts that were more similar to battle wounds. He lay prostrate on a mattress made of empty solemness. He dug holes into his soul praying someone would fill his voids. Yet, he didn't really know how to pray. Instead, he repeated practiced redundancies hoping someone heard him scream with urgency, *PLEASE HELP ME!*

Yet Silence begets silence...   and it all muffled his destiny.

This little boy was dying and no one would come to his rescue. So this little boy had to discover how to tend to his own wounds.

He was left mangled - a hideous atrocity - yet, if you look for his disfigurement I promise you wouldn't see...   This little boy cried on the inside and was flooding internally and left little room for his feelings so he wore his emotions on his sleeve.

This little boy choked on his insecurities cause he wasn't taught to swallow things like his pride and he never understood why they called them memories. Cause he remembered everything as if life was stuck on repeat.

This little boy followed the wrong path cause for a minute the road to death seemed a little more pleasing.

This little boy thought accolades and self- humiliating behavior would make life more easy.

This little boy was poisoned by pornography and thought love was spelled S-E-X, so he tried to repeat the things he would see.

This little boy was lonely and would constantly talk to strangers because at least they heard him speak

This little boy still survives - although he tried to die repeatedly. I'll introduce you to this little boy because he still resides inside of me.

I'm this little boy - nice to meet you.

So let my life be the example to boys left crying in their bedrooms.

Let my tears wage wars against the cowardly attacks of a generation of men who were crippled in the molding designed so perfect but as life began sculpting it left the image they're worthless.

And let my prayers cast dreams to the visionless and hopeless bound, blind in their past now - their freedom is the focus!

Let my actions lay a path to a road so narrow - not paved in good intentions, but laid with persecutions and cemented in redemption

And let Salvation be distributed so freely that the number of souls coming to Christ match the homeless and the needy

So Jesus let me be an example! Regardless if I'm youthful. I remember my first real poem: I sat at the computer while my tears stroked the keyboard the pain unlayered within the stanzas and my anger lashed out in metaphors. But then I encountered God...

So for my past...

This little boy won't cry anymore.

INSPIRE

Excuse me, can I have your attention, please?

I have been pondering this for a minute now

So I hope that you are listening

When is the last time you measured your effort and found room to go harder?

Took inventory of your drive and tried to go further?

We have lived life like green insects for too long

Crept and crawled

Slithered and slothed

Our way into barely gustation

Nibbled piece by piece

Carried volcanos of potential but they dwelled in dormancy

See your table has been prepared with a seat

And now it's time to eat

Indulge yourself into the process of victory

Dive into wells of deeper energy

Bite down, better yet, put hands to plow

And refuse to turn backwards

Can you feel it?

There's something changing

Are you willing to bear down and hold on until bones break and joints dislocate?

Are you willing to press straight until sweat breaks and soil saturates and your cocoon-like shell prepares to hold its weight?

Take the front seat into your ENDLESS DESTINY!

Get on your feet and prepare to change your story.

PURPOSE

To look at life, mistakes, and past

At dreams deferred, yet hope outlasts

To fight for those who fight alone

To risk yourself to see them strong

To mend the hearts of broken souls

To enlighten those who live unexposed

To press beyond the pain you feel

To live for truth and by His will

To know one day that you will win

And they who doubt will then repent

Your journey is to sacrifice

To see a world live their best life

A story not like fairytale

A way to love even thru' hell

To leave behind your legacy

A changin' world thru' his belief

HIDE AND SEEK

I ran from a place that I never knew was created for me

Childhood massacred by martyred relationships that set the precedent

For Liberty

Tag team to my innocence hidden in the cascades of the tree

Shadows that covered me

I ran from truth that light conceived

And called it *hide and seek*

Memories of mistakes overwhelmed in isolation

Honesty and reputation played handball with which deserved to be sacrificed

I lived life in the middle

Making quick escapes when reality became too real

I couldn't truly hide in the first place

I ran cuz I was darker still

It wasn't until I realized the light was enlightening still

Explode me from the threshold of my solitude expose the truth

That society desired to keep my darkness drowned

And this genocide is proof

So hold me accountable to my truths released from lips

Hold me responsible for the burdens of a battered race

I'll keep my hands up just to bear the cross of every forgotten black face

How many tears must saturate the soil before we finally grow the courage to do something

I represent the broken

The misguided collection who were promised liberties that we still pay the price in body bags for

I share the same heartbeats as those put to arrest when they came to arrest

They put six in his chest

Tell me is it fair I'm forced to instill in my children warning thoughts that warning shots may come for just a warning

I decree I am covered in His blood filled with Holy Ghost and love

Yet how many slain lambs must it take until they've sacrificed enough

Ripped at our heritage and hung it from a tree

Stuck spikes in Christ's arms and hung'em so they can see

They traded us death for love and told us that we are free

Yet they run from the tag of justice bearing not guilty on their sleeve

Hiding from Persecution

Now let's call that *hide and seek*

The enemy has poisoned our prophets

Made mute the mouths of the mighty

But why scream for help to the deaf

They gave us road maps to our safety

Yet placed in detours to our death

Grand theft to our destiny like it was automatic

Our safety seems to have semi the value as theirs

Here's my license I don't care

Take four from this semi-Automatic

While our children all watch it happen

You've served us your hatred

And I do not feel protected by the hands of man

Thank God my life was never in their hands to begin with

Jesus took the wheel a long time ago

It's my job to ensure that I become a vessel to bondaged souls

Freedom never came independently declared

It was a son who was slain whose inheritance he shared

If we truly want change we better start there!
For the Oscars and Trayvon's and Freddie's who can't speak
And the Altons and philandos and mikes left bleeding
in the street
We can fight with our fists scream no justice no peace
But if hate fills your heart then how free could you be
It's action in love and entrust in the King
You can't hide from His truth but you'll find him if you seek

THIS LITTLE'S THREE LITTLE

Have you ever seen how tornado winds sweep away everything

It reminds me of pains whose memory makes me squeal

They play backdrop to scenes of nightmares

Stormy nights where tree limbs

Kept rhythms onto windows that mirrored

The sound of cracked leather

Grandfather clocks ticked in slow motion

And echoed in hallways that played red carpet to my doorway

Me: Hiding in closets of straw bedrooms

Tears made lake like puddles in the dust of my hopes

Muddied my vision

Fear creaked it's way towards my entrance

I could hear you howling from a distance

Your screams still make me shiver

Each bellow huffed and puffed terror into my soul

No door could withstand your bark

No bark could fence in your bite

I ducked into shadows for sanctuary

Yet you still blew down the house that night

Your beating left me pink

scared my meat

Burnt my skin fried me deep

I can still fill the heat

Made me beg: "will this bake end"

I concede my defeat

I ran ahead to fortress from your fury

Hoping this gate would protect me

My cries couldn't create a moat large enough

So my anger began investing

I'd hammer hate into the walls of my heart

Trying to keep what was left in

I tried to walk the plank of my own demise

But could never make it overboard

So these 4x4s would border in the four corners of my mind

I waited and you knocked this time

Attempted to hide your hideous snarl

And convince me to let you inside

I smothered my pain with a mask of shame

Yet i refused to cry

I saw the anger in your eyes as you clawed for my throat

You thundered to the sky until my walls shook and broke

I broke again like every dusk before

I laid in a mixture of blood and slop

I can still see you at my door

I can smell the alcohol in your exhales

Feel the regret in your heartbeat

Hear the slurred whimpering in your salutations

Taste my bloodied reminder of the pain that comes with full moons

I knew you would return soon

I knew my body, a temple, wasn't prepared for this truth

These battered bricks couldn't play barricade from this lone wolf's abuse

I needed a bunker

Safe zone for my refuge

Asylum from the awaiting silence:

Theme music to my confessed doom

Confused at how a howl hauls me into

This broken space

How I tried to renovate my self confidence a thousand ways

It always just crumbles in the end

How I still quake to your scowl

The glitch in my adulthood

Yet now, when you hear my roar

You can tell i was baptized in monsoons that scattered wolf-packs

Left them to fend for themselves

Marred whatever was in their way

Barked and bit with equal ferocity

Carnivorously disheartened the innocent

Always drew first blood

And Took territories

one little squeal at a time

The Teen

On Courts and fields he made them proud
His name they'd chant and shout out loud
Yet when the game was done
Whether they lost or won
He'd then return to his dark house

See where he's from he always stood out
They reprimand and say shut your mouth
At school they're cruel
Daily ridiculed
The darkest spot seen in the crowd

One day he thought had a plan
He'd take the matters into his hands
Aimed for his wrists
Thank God he missed
Now this Teen can meet the Man

YOUNG MAN

You have the world in front of you there's no need to rush

You have been eager for attention and someone else's touch

I know his pain is getting to you and his violence has been rough

But give yourself some time because I promise you don't have enough

Father's constant beatings

Mother's absent and mean

Abuse is what you've been raised in so you think it's what you need

Don't let the sharpness of the pain leave the scars upon your wrist

Don't let the secrets in her body get you trapped between her hips

I know it looks pleasing and she's promised you the world

And your body is feeling different cause she is not like other girls

The truth is she knows this and she's banking on the fact

That you will overlook the issue and the eight year age gap

I promise if you focus on your future and not when you all will meet

You will avoid abusive cycles and becoming slave to more back seats

See you're gambling with your career and I know you're only seventeen

But 25 is where it starts, and the next will be forty

I know you think it's fine and you'll brag to your friends

But the path you are headed, I know where it will end

They see you as an object, get their fill and then discard

You want love that can fill voids while they just want you to stay hard

You will go from one to another - you're underage, but they are smart

You desire a mother's touch so they keep playing the part

Every game that she missed - they always showed up

Every time she refused to hug - they always wanna cut

You will think it's not an issue but they are messing with your mind

This drug will become your addiction and you will want it all the time

Everywhere you will go you will have it - sometimes no matter who it's from

You will lose scholarships and your career - just to get your fun

You will think you are winning because of the notches on your belt

But your rep will be destroyed and you won't have very much left

You will finally get control but the price will cost a lot

You can kiss your sports goodbye and the future you may have thought

The way that you look at things will change at 25

Cuz now you are responsible for caring for a life

You have so many talents and you will learn to love again

You will finally gain back trust and truly have real friends

The life you'll have is different but there is purpose in it too

I had to search for it the hard way to finally find the Truth

The Fact is there is still hope, no matter what you choose

But don't let them take your innocence because that belongs to you

DEAR FATHER,

As I close my eyes the only sound you can hear is my heart as it pulsates

I'm nervous now heavy panting palms sweating deep breaths I take

And I search the hidden shadows of my mind

Searching through lock doors and corridors of things I've locked away for some time

So let's revisit these memories of scars made from hard times

And let's reopen the floodgates of tears dammed up because I built bridges over lakes of pain

You see I knew I'd drown if I tried to swim through
So somehow I had to make a way

God forgive me for asking, but why was my life this way? Why can't I remember if he spent more time with the bottle or his hand to my face? Why do I remember lonely conversations to my dad that I hid
inside a closet marked, *disappointment*? There, I open boxes filled with heartache wrapped in, "*we tried to make it work for the kids' sake.*"

My mother's cries combined with the "*I hate you's,*" *and* "*You cheated on me for the last time...*"
Dad, she never left you.
You manipulated her to believe that you'd change and of course, the kids believed too

But you never did...
In between jail time and rehab
You left just enough space for my life
To be a living hell! - Thanks for the gift, dad.

Next to that, was a shelf filled with,
"*I wish you could have been there,*"
When I took the knife to my wrist...
But thank God that I missed!
You never knew about this,
You never asked...

You see I have a room of depression...
On the walls are trophies and awards
Cuz that's what came to matter

My drawers filled with alcohol bottles,
Opened up and poured out
The abused body and soul
You see, my life had no control...

I lay on a bed of addiction, loneliness and a cold heart caused me
to retreat to these positions

You see, my covers have no restrictions;
This is where my safe zone meets my ambitions
My capability to dream never stopped by inhibitions

It's like my pillow could narrate the story of my struggle and
every tear squeezed from it fills my hallowed heart with a puddle

And this is supposed to be my sanctuary - but I can't escape home
movie's recording

The terrors hiding in the darkness
I can't run from the beatings - I mean,
In God's eyes, whose fault is this?

You see I don't blame you, but you,
you are apart of this

You swing, I scream
But you tell me it's the alcohol that makes you mad
You sober up and sit me down
and say you'll try and be a better dad

We exchange *I love you's* and go on about our day and eight years
my own senior
It took me now to find a way

You see my pain brought forth strength.
Eyes open, tears fallen
I allow my head to meet my hands
I cried through all this
I found God so he saved me in the end

You see, you taught me what not to be
 and on God I must depend
And now dad - Now, I am a man.

Sincerely your Son,
Brandon Christopher Allen

DEAR MOTHER,

(This poem comes at a heavy cost that took me three decades to accrue.)

This is not the first thing I penned you,
but this probably holds the most truth.

I can still hear whispers of lullabies from lips that seemed to have
pecked my doom

Insanity plee and insane I must be for being the crazy seed that
infected her womb

For a long time I blamed myself.
 Took responsibility for being the cause of your torment...
Like the breaking of your water-boarded
 you in so tight it felt like drowning
I understand that you did what you needed to swim
Disconnected from the weight that sunk you
You never expected to be the kayak that kept us afloat

I always felt like the captain to the ship of torture that overturned
in mixed emotions.
Abandoned on an island of isolation -
 solitude became my refuge.

Slit risk, survival kit while trying to lifeboat my own rescue
Drowning in oceans of intoxication and strangled by habits, I was
forced to choke down depression and grow up in madness.

Mom, Have you ever seen a tree grow in darkness?
It doesn't.

It barely sprouts and its roots are crippled.
Machine guns massacred my youth
And we all took turns at the trigger.
          Terrorist attacks on my existence
My face turned to a trigger.

My smile was the stale reminder that hers had been frequently
incarcerated.
I was his twin, shared the same eyes nose and skin
We both had to be incubated
I six hours, he six times.

I never knew how much time he spent inside
You always made the transition out easy.
The walls were cold here too

It is hard to blame you because you always tried to mend this
jailbird house each time he flew the coup.

You forgot how peacock you were.
No matter how many eyes were on you.

I can only remember tears escaping your eyes twice.
Anger was a familiar tool

Mother, you always told me you weren't there for the abuse, but
the truth is that's when I needed you.

When shadows haunted my walls, and wouldn't let me escape my
room. I hid Inside a closet marked *disappointment.*
There I open boxes filled with *heartache,*
wrapped in, *you-tried-to-make-it-work-for-the-kids'-sake.*

Your angry cries combined with the "*I hate you's*"
You cheated on me for the last time.

It was hard for you to leave his noose
He manipulated you to believe that he'd change
and of course the kids did too
        But he never did.

And you didn't really make it easy
In between jail time and rehab tries
There left just enough space for my life to be a living hell; Thanks
for the gift guys!

Next to that was a shelf filled with
I wish you could have been there
when I took the knife to my wrist...

I wonder if you really believe the seed that you spent
Time and energy with- who felt he was the issue
Would take matters into his own hands to make sure it didn't
exist

I wonder...*Mother,*
if you see the man today as a man today.
Or if you still stare out of pain scarred glasses
containing tears that have been begging for their freedom.
Do you still see me wallowing in a pool of my mistakes
or have you taken notice that I have yet to drown?
Do you consider the part you played
how much difference presence over provision
would have truly made?
Do you half wish my life was at a different place?
 Do you even remember the one you dropped me off at?

Mother, I have come to accept the fullness of my
disappointments!
I have made moments of misery last longer than necessary and
have taken you along for the ride.

Yet, I am still getting used to having both hands on the wheel.
I will not wreck my destiny and I have long forgiven you for the
detours -
I just hope one day
you'll forgive yourself.

Your Son,
Brandon Christopher Allen

SAM I AM

I never questioned if you were genuine

I never doubted your motives

I was slave to you bound to the whim of your desires

My heart was conquered you ran through my blood streams

your venom I was left toxic

I lost truth in fact I replaced it with you

We laid in the garden and found out we were nude yet Being

covered I'd never choose

I'd often visit your vacuum and you'd seal my values inside of

your womb

And I'd reply I love you too

I've never been more confused

See I crawl onto lost stages designed by my muse

And there My poetry battered and abused

it cries onto mic stands

Stories of how I left sticky notes on night stands

Reminding myself about different parts of my identity that

have been stolen by my own hands

You took the best of me yet I always get up and offer you more

And you relentlessly withdrew from What I've stored a

And I fear that you knew better; I mean you at least knew that

I would never

Stop sipping from your poison

As long as you'd offer me more

Temptress your tempting terror has tricked me

I allowed your hands to stroke me into misery

Castrate away my strength

And I became spectacle for the weak

The unpretentious and the meek

You sought out the root of my power

And I gave it to you with ease

I kept kept flirting with the deathly

Twice I avoided disaster but if u constantly drink her elixir

Then whom truly is the master?

So if I die before you remember this poem scribed into grails of

ancient that will last into eternal

The parable of how I surrendered as I laid between your lap

For the liar in Delilah is how I fell into this trap

Signed,

Seeking After Mercy

SAM(son)

APB

Our girls are still missing

We know where they've last been seen

Walking the streets of America

Abducted from their everyday routines

Home of the brave and land of the free

Yet at its capitol, you must live in fear if you're a colored teen

Imagine sending your daughter out into her day to Accomplish dreams

For us to only return to a nightmare

Urgency isn't strong enough of a word to

Describe our suffering

Our babies are having their magic stolen by tricks Smuggled into vans that fast-laned their pureness

Forced to abandon safety drowning in a sea of absence,

and our hands can't reach far enough to retrieve them

Where are the lifeboats?

Little girls coerced into grown woman by the hands of Beast who have a taste for royalty

Yet we've been labeled savage

and our girls are still missing

I wonder if you placed side to side the photos of a black Man and our lost queens

One stolen innocence other proposed guilty

Who would be found the quickest?

I imagine them uniformed and crying to the heavens like a mass choir

Smiles beacon like a lighthouse

Eyes glimmer like moon-lakes

Feet pattering frantically to a beat of each lost day they grow more distant

Screams harmonically pitch perfect to the acapella of their forced wandering sisters

Left to fend for their own sanity

Blinded by the pain they bring, yet they've brailled their own healing

Made in the image of eternity

Resilience branded to the backbone of their generations

Tattooed to their DNA they are born survivors

Made to last

Driven by the faith and fortitude fenced by fortress fixed to their future forging their freedom

Our girls are still missing

Yet they don't need to be found again

They are stitched into every part of world history

I can feel them in the air I breathe

They are the foundation of our legacy

The perfection in every masterpiece

Look to the skies the stars constellate their destiny

Angels of protection have been sent as reinforcements

Special Ops in the spirit

Search and rescue in the harshest conditions

Purple Heart these soldiers

because they are true heroes

Brown skin...

Teenage...

and still missing...

The Man

To introduce a man of the wild
The tarnished bronze of a golden child
Though his dreams exist
We'd be remiss
To ignore how he beguiled

Convinced the world to trust his smile
Yet this broken man hid all the while
Promises unkept
Without much left
He lived in his denial

Something he knew had to change
For death was ringing out his name
His soul at risk
Of the darkest midst
Filled with regret and Shame

CONVERSATIONS WITH A POET

I was once told, *"Don't ever be afraid to be vulnerable."*

And I was told *"life without love wasn't worth living"*...

These are conversations with a poet and I responded by saying:

Love never showed me its reflection.

It hid behind summer days and steamed covered mirrors.

It played hide and seek with every heart that I encountered - mine included.

It was stolen like an old western robbery, "Hands up", in the midst of horse trampled dust.

It was manipulated, premanufactured...

It was the child born from society's adulterated affair with media.

Birth defects ignored caused us to diagnose love.

We have prescribed pills of, *"sex is how I love you,"* taken twice daily.

We gave it pills of *'Please dress in as little self-esteem as possible; I promise they'll notice...'*

Culture kamikaze bombed itself into where I harbored pearls of love's definition.

Poisoned were these feelings...

I was once told, *"Don't ever be afraid to be vulnerable."*

I was told that life without love wasn't worth living.

But why offer transparency to a generation built on the backs of liars?

How can I? When social media has perverted the world's eyes so much that I don't even feel comfortable posting my daughter dancing.

What love is this that we have to question its reciprocation?

Have you ever imagined where love hides when you can't find it?

Well I searched, 'Lost n' Found' - and found myself digging through phone books.

Searching returned texts... hoping love would arrive to the sound of doorbells and be waiting on my doorstep.

Instead, found that love is playing *ding-dong-ditch*... Yes, I'm in love but *you* are still missing.

I wonder if Webster has anxiety attacks thinking maybe he left out the true definition?

See, *true love* was created in perfection...

Molded with the perfect kiss from springtime's lips

and sealed with summer reflections...

Sunshine bright like a newborn's first breath...

Eyes wide - you are beauty like a butterfly in first flight...

Colors so majestic on kaleidoscope wingspans

You are destination dreamed

Yet not quite seen...

You are *passion*, blood flow to limbs like roller coaster rides...

You are *masterpiece painted* in the exhales of each breath I take of you...

Until it becomes so overwhelming I suffocate

I'm asthmatic to an atmosphere that the world says you don't belong in.

Lungs tightened... I mean, how can you breathe if you subtract the creator of the oxygen? So allow me to inhale you like my life depends on it...

You are *freedom* - like adolescent bike rides - post-training wheels.

Love never felt so intoxicating!

I'm addicted to the Rolodex of stashed away memories of our encounters.

I'm unconscious to my love-sick of missing you from each time we hung over this.

I'm allergic to your absence, so vomit my regrets of not telling you my truth.

Beauty isn't worthy enough of a definition to describe you.

Love just taps the surface...

I want to excavate into these mountains of emotions - skydive into feelings that describe my daydreams...

Happily-Ever-After finally found its way home

Aromas of fresh dew set each day gives me another opportunity...

Conversations so fluent you could play them backwards and still need no translation...

Making statements like : *If you just listened to me talk you'd swear I did poetry...*

Heartbeats to the sound of time clicking away as we finger-paint our eternity together

We are vulnerable...

This is love.

FAITH CONFESSION

I've inscribed destiny to my chest so as heartbeats Under mirrored
reflections I'm reminded this is what I live for
I was born to be enslaved
Bound by my own imperfections
I was filthy

Wrapped in rags of sins that my father chose for me
I dead man walking would slit wrists to departed Freedoms
hoping that the numbness would go away
Fingertips I couldn't feel them would grab for the Minutes of my
life I've wasted
Spilled was my blood incomparable to the blood of the savior
I was in the fields covered from head to toe
In my past
Yet I waited for suns to set
and moons to rise
Just so I could remember
That you can find light in the darkness

I wondered if I stayed consistent enough
Regardless of how secluded I was
Would Samuel still call for me and anoint me, king!
I wanna trade my rags for your riches
See I fiend for iniquities injected death
Into every part of my existence
Rehab me please.
Burn this flesh and meat ill to cold turkey
If you withdrawal from me these impurities

Maestro conduct this sinner's symphony
Until it crescendos into redemption
I wanna be filled with sonnets of salvations
Let me utter monologues of your praises
Tasting - like heaven on my lips

Yet I've still justified my actions

you said, *knock and you would answer*
Yet I refuse to show up to your address
So in this address, I'll address
How I address you...

Dear Father,
There's significance in my communication to you. Let not mere
words take precedence over power in relationship. I wanna
be submerged in your presence. Let angelic encounters be like
whispers that sing love songs to the purpose inside of me.
No longer do I desire the status quo of complacency, meshed with
modern religiosity, that allowed me to paint my own pictures of
what my savior should be for me.

My American idol need not audition the people already chosen.
And this image was my victor. Satan stood in ovation as I
furthered from fulfillment,
but God put an end to my destructions. Popularity and the Voice
is what killed it.

See I discovered what faith is. I face blindly in the opposite
direction. Others project noise - but me, being your sheep,
recognize your sound - then make my selection!

I choose you because you first chose me!
See this is no regular piece.
This is a call-to-attention!
Where we have taken marching orders
as common suggestions
This is your identity paper mashed with
Your mistakes and your refusal to forgive yourself Sin covered In
paint so magnificent
That it glitters and sparkles in the sunlight
But regardless of its beauty
It's still hollow on the inside

Let us reflect more like piñatas
Because even as we are beaten, swung at, and Taken for granted
Our purpose, as we swing from the tree of life,

Broken and split open
Still spews out the prize
And regardless of what we think, when others arrive and see, we piñatas,
It brings joy to their eyes!

This is prayer. This is an assignment to the tongue that you have given us to move masses and create access.
Open doors with open mouthes, your voice spews out. See, we speak a common language.

This means war!
And we'll battle with a sword of revelation
As we speak cherubims from heaven
Engage in combat with minions of Satan
Davids of all nations
Collect pebbled victories
and slingshots of defeat
to each Goliath in front of them
Screaming...
Who dares to defy the armies of my Lord?!
Please choose me.
I'll show them.

Meek and humble with heavenly rumbles in his belly
and from his loins and heritage
Birth the seed of salvation!

And even death tried to trap it
but his spirit is the key to unlock masses
And his blood red sees Egypt is getting faster
But this part is where faith carries you
to a longitude of promise and a latitude of land
Weary then mount wingspans
Seeking then climb mountains

We can hide blindly behind facades of shame
but still encounters with true freedom
Will demask us - and change our names

THE IN BETWEEN

We live in a world of misconception where we let complacent ideals become our parables. We teach, *Work smarter not harder*, yet we work for a little more than nothing.
We expect our cake with a side of ice cream and we dare not share it. We became a people of handouts and hand-me-downs tryna figure out the quickest route with the least amount effort. We are the hook up kings skilled in bootlegging, and I'll guarantee we don't cherish things.

We say, *'A bird in the hand is better than two the bush.'* See, this story has been falsified. I mean, how could this be true because if you provide enough feed - the birds will come to you!
But this generation has suffered from silly satirical circumstances. We accepted being accepting of receiving crumbs from the master's table. Yet we serve too many masters. Our reality is jaded. We look through glasses darkly shaded to a light that has been faded.

We've put blinders to our destiny. We've walked paths of forgotten struggles causing ourselves to repeat history and her story and the fables of generations that we've lost in translation. We've become a number. A statistical tally mark to societal judgments. We've fallen victim to the failures of our bloodline and we've lost conviction.
And I'm the sample of this census
I remember conversation that began with poor spotted colored lips that were cracked like front Porch wooden steps
Parting with exhales of small creaks getting louder the closer I get to entry.
Mirrors played handball with each swipe of self-esteem that lost in competition
With voices in my head reminding that hatred wore masks of children's faces
I was born in a city overpopulated by the fact that I didn't belong there
I sat in elementary classrooms identified with the alias *"you know, the black kid"*

And I stood as the spot in class pictures clicking heels together repeating, *There's no place like home* rooms; never felt so unwelcome...

Age ten is when I discovered that facades came in all sizes. I could play Two-face and trick them to believe me Carve manufactured grins into my melancholy cheeks until they laughed with me exclaiming, *what a joker!*

I used to daydream waking up Xi, to injections from theses poison IVs- escaping to where no one can see my dark nights.

I wish I could have been my own superhero...
Yet I fell victim to the villain inside of me.
Depression consumed the better half of me
Excrete tears in forms of razor blades that somehow didn't cut too deep. My insecurities arrested me and charged me with *Attempted Murder* and I was my only witness - yet I never pled guilty.

Innocence doesn't belong here. It was split from me like broken families. I became a foster child to my reality. Beaten like life wasn't for me.

Force fed maturity on a plate of sexuality - they told me I can't move from the table until I finish servings of sex. Is the answer *swallow your morals?* I promise the death I just served you is nutritious. Look at me I'm filled with vitamin D and I had enough to go around.

Have you ever built your own pedestal turn platform for public demise? Ridicule turned punch lines - He said he changed, what a lie!

Age 25, birthed in the world was my everything. Wrapped in cloths of shame and self torturing.
I still hear the voices scream. I thought you were saved Typical Christian thing.
Fallen to the typical hidden sin...
Depression went down a little easier than facing them so I'll

rebuild my stage again on pride and ignorance　　　Knock two
times and I'll point you In the direction of my emptiness
Welcome to the black hole of my existence.
This void in between death and living.
The space in between chasing your dreams and never wanting to
awaken.
The space in between True love's heartbeats and　　　　　I beat
you because I love you.

The place in between innocence and corruption
The place in between the right leg of insecurities and the left of
this is how he showed he loved me...
The place in between fatherhood and fatherless where
households laid stage for your reenacted torment

the In between and I lived here

But I refused to remain
Resilient became attached to my name tattooed to the Backbone
that I was forced to grow
in between the wings
fly into the arms of your destiny it's waiting
Meditate daily. I promise it will make you stronger.

War in between sunset and the moonrise watch
Faith tilt the playing field in your direction
Time stands stil.l
Please leave your past insecurities behind
I left the stage just so he can use my shoulders to bear crosses
I took flame to my name
My reputation no longer relevant
He recreated my story
So judge me, I dare you. I still have the evidence.
Surgery is in progress, It just has a face lift.　　　Please, can
you tell me - do I look like Jesus yet?

I closed every door I had open to all I was seeking
Then he opened gates to heavenly entries
He said run forests filled with living trees

Fruits that leave seeds sown into the valley
Climb onto this mountain
I promise I will meet you there
Slavery is where you started - freedom is your promise
Moses go back and free the people
They will be waiting in between

MY HYPOCRISY

Hypocrisy intertwined with promises of liberty we purge ourselves deliberately issuing false advertisement and the marketing of misery were addicts and drug choice is ignorance so intelligence is enemy almost as if it's the sin in me I mean you're seriously believing me and these four walls pews and podium is the means from which I am delivering

Welcome to the church

And I'll be the first to exclaim how we have malnourished the body diseased its identity

Fingerprints carved from skin so AID's the death to our immunity

And we preach healer but too wretched to receive it

Blood shed redemption - hoarded and distributed as we see pleasing

Judgments necessary just to say if you are deserving

Gavel slammed the ruling's dammed regardless if you earned it

From the pews or the jury spews the fire from which their burning

Chants of condemnation, perfect replacement for scriptures our children are learning

And we part-time Christians are on the clock trying to earn our holy raises

Like a Sunday morning praises means we are getting bonuses on a paycheck

And it's funny how we treat this as validation for six days of a living heathen

Living with that Peter Syndrome Pretend we don't know JESUS

But what we've just done is stained his reputation. We clothed ourselves in Christianity and soiled on His Glory WE have defamed his name by attaching it to ours claiming our one-way ticket so we can see the Lord   Yet most people wouldn't trust the train that you're getting on or me

We take advantage of the father screaming, "Lord you're just so forgiving!"

HE replies back, "I am but that doesn't mean just keep sinning!"

Yet we do and he screams, " I want you." And we said, " Lord me too, but she's so cute. So I may slip once or twice but Lord make me new."

It's ironic how we use God any way that we choose

Even though Christ cursed the tree from the root for producing sour fruit.

Again welcome to the church and this seats for you.

Here's a list of prayers hallelujahs and scriptures too!

And if you ever get confused, just fake it like we do!

Its sad, and i'm tired. Tired of this continuous behavior. Cycles of hellish activitiesbrewed in waters so warm that it's bound to be spewed through his teeth.

We are a generation chosen; yet, we cower to the call. We allow media, music, and moguls to mold us and we're worshipping them all.

Like we were made in Oprah's image and we bow to the feet of Jay and Beyonce; like they came to save us and we pray in *Love and Hip Hop's* name

We feeling oh, so *Insecure* and just *being Mary Jane*

We still *Breaking Bad* into *Scandal's* gates

To give a *Fast and Furious* praise

I mean in this *Game of Thrones* whose *Empire* do

You give *Power* to anyway?!

How quickly we mistake the face of our savior until we're in need - showing up to heaven's gates like invitation was received. Jesus answers and replies like, *"Excuse me. Do you know me? I think you have the wrong address because this is invite only."*

See that road to hell is lonely...

So I dare you, no, I beg you!

Relinquish this mainstream Christianity poisoned by this mesh with media popularity and build a real relationship with Jesus and his spirit. Allow it to give you clarity until salvation becomes a treasure that you will never share sparingly.

R IS FOR ROMANCE

I tell stories. I am author to a photographic memory illustrator to innocence crippled in perversion

I am writer dictator to dictation I am head of stead prepared to address the nation

This is poetry.

Eyes closed, I envision our first encounter like mother with newborn;I never wanted you to leave except to hold you closer.

I dreamed of you - nightly rendezvouses in a room I marked private - do not disturb signs made it clear that we were preoccupied. I enjoyed our alone time.

We masqueraded about. I was so full of passion you never let me forget how important you were to me. Reminders came in the form of your absence, where voids would play tricks on my loneliness.

This is where I first understood that separation doesn't always make you miss the person. It's scary that even though I loved you I was quick to desire a replacement when I wasn't patient enough for your return.

I realized LOVE is spoken every language yet somehow we still require a translator.

We were pure when we were together but somehow my sanctuary was infected by desolation.

It started with simple rejection calls. Then unanswered knocks. Unanswered then grew into an abnormal and uncontrollable mass! See, love turned to cancer.

Darkness birthed division then married to abandonment then they bred an army and their first son was Goliath and he declared himself my personal giant.

And his favorite game was hide and seek and he'd always find me then hide my destiny until I quit trying.

Love lived here; no longer. It became scrapbooks of times spent blurred. Images while under the influence of destruction...

i wrote you a letter many times over but always returned to

sender. See, my love I knew was still existing but I couldn't recall where they were living.

I was truly lost but no one knew I was missing.

This is the fairy tale of lusts captivity though I'm no Prince Charming, I sought my damsel in distress.

As my regrets grew into replacements for an unforeseen kiss.

In bondage, I became slave man to the lands' authority My debt unpaid left me for ransom

Until the king paid my transgressions with a worthy collateral

Freedom never felt so good. Love never looked like this.

I transcribed on me these love stories until I became its reflection.

Love no longer just defined as temporary escapes to imagination's paradise . See, we were One defined two make hearts grow closer, and if three times is a charm we need no four leaf clover! And 5 o'clock shadows couldn't hover over the six days it took for creation on 7 we'll rest endless, because 8 may be lucky but I'm sure it's filled with new beginnings and I pray cloud 9 gets me closer to u in the end. Just to walk into your presence   see your perfect 10!

The lover is the light and overabundance ventricles pumping equal to none and this R?...Well, this R is for romance!

CHURCH PEW CHRONICLES

We both entered here with the same idea in our mind
To worship until our worries of unworthiness are Wiped clean
Slates of our mistakes made pristine
Yet yours still carry smudges of your indiscretions
Wooden doors cracked open like heaven's gates and the sun
painted a welcome sign
In the floor of the lobby
Yet their looks lacked love

I, more vocal, polk-a-dotted my appearance with Pretentious
praise!
You, hidden behind the plexiglass mask
You painted it in a fresh coat of
Cocoa colored pigment
They could see your two faces-
Hidden behind the cigarette-stained, white painted fence of teeth
that chain-linked within it your reality

 Your breath carried the scent of your sins
They recognized it immediately as did I
I just gargled repentance before entering

I can tell by the smell of ridicule
you were perfumed by your past so the last place you came to
rain dance made you praise to ballads of rejection

Your handclaps match the rhythm of the soul drums
Your pain strummed like the bassline
Strained tears fell like springtime
To the sound of keys,
Like strings of wind chimes

Hoping to enrich the black soil of your tarnished reputation
The one you so conveniently covered with the Perfect green sod
of your *Sunday's Best*

I do my best not to notice but it looks, oh so familiar
Forced to feather fraud with fear
I mean fear forces frauds down the row
Closer to the exit

I can see your lips lined with insecurities
It shows through their quiver
They have more shakes then maracas
More shakes than rattle and
These slimy hypocritical snakes
Have bitten at your Apple

You stand on Withered ankles
Arthritic from running
In silent circles of your secrets
Carrying the wretched weight of your self-hate

Your ears pierced by the sounds of salty snickers And taunting
fairy tales of dreams
Wet of unfulfillment

Ears dangling, glistening
Whispers of broken promises
Dipped in gold
Yet, hallow at its core
You have been filling your heart with bits of hope Only to still see
the glass empty
Yet men like me, thirsty,
 Still see there's enough to drink!

You were counted as prey
As soon as you took your seat
Your sound smothered by shadows of solitude Sinfully strangled
silent
Saturated in sepia
Like old blood soiled sheets
Surgically siphoned from your soul
Slit to separate you from your serial survival
Yet survival is the song that you sing

Yet, sometimes the church
Just hasn't played the right melody!
They force you into another key
We have forced premature exits to baby sheeps
Then judge their wolf bites
Your life isn't made to be inspected just protected Covered and comforted, not rejected
Mended and molded, not manipulated
We love the church and will celebrate it
And we are the same people
Who will cause the world to hate it
Church Pew Chronicles

MAGIC AND MEMORIES

I remember nights when tears fell like rainstorms

in the streetlight, and happiness would hide in dark corner, and in back alleys. Cracks in the sidewalks were mirrored by heartache that was etched in my existence.

I remember nights filled with lustful interaction:

This is where body kisses, back scratches, and soft skins and deep passion

compensated for the memories instilled from a threatened soul and belt lashings.

I became one with my sin. My sexual immoralities became my means to say, "*I love you*"

but I couldn't even love myself...

I recall damp sheets in black rooms with white walls Cold sweats from hot nights.

Long moans and loud shouts

left with short-lived pleasure and silent cries.

Voids of lowliness were filled with multiple visitors to the room of shadows.

Quick escapes and sudden exits were

followed by arms stretched to

grab at the empty space.

Lock doors shut in screams from pure terror.

Soft sounds seep through small openings too large. Places, yet, I still couldn't reach you.

I dream of days before the hard-times

Days where I didn't have to revisit the memories

of the nights prior.

Days where I couldn't trace the whelps down my body and scars didn't make crossroads with each other.

I dreamt of the good times.

The times where light would drink gourd the darkness making way for this runaway train.

Tubman my tragedy.

Turn buried eulogy into roadmap.

I remember that secret place where wretchedness couldn't dwell and its tempting demeanor couldn't slither in my solemness.

It's like a barrier orighteousness around me cupping my external, gripped ever so securely.

I wonder if this is what heaven feels like.

Absent of cocooned uncertainty...

Winged with faith...

Patterned for purpose...

Unique to one design...

I remember the dark times.

I remember the nights that tears fell like rainstorms

in the street lights

Yet this time - I brought an umbrella.

This time, I refuse to be held hostage by a memory to only recall life as a caterpillar.

I live above the torment!

Butterfly as high as my potential...

Pass my limits!

Past can't limit!

Even when those dark nights try to ask for a visit,

I remember that these are only memories.

Incantations of harbored hallucinations trying to cast spells on my mind.

I remember my light is too miracle for this dark magic
I remember that I turned out fine.
I remember that I am not bound to repeat these motion pictures.
I remember that I am not bound at all.
I remember that...
I
Am
Free

POETICALLY ADORNED

I've never been one to be good at intimacy
I've always been good with my words

Created playgrounds on brittle half-truths
Swirling slides to my own demise
Stairways to hearts where bridges of fragmented Manipulation
left you tangled
In my jungle gym of hope
In this jaded reality
I would leave you
Bruised, blacktop and blue

I swore I had more to offer
Yet I was really running on fumes
Wore costumes that gave the illusion I had it together
I chalked the picture I wanted you to see
This was war of my identity
And I forced you to be a pow

Fed you just enough so you could survive
My love was cruel and unusual
I tortured you with lies
I gave you minimal light
And the isolation from real truth
Kept you thirsting after this water board
D-Day has been inescapable since Adam bomb
So nuclear, it left generations cursed to this fallout
I'm still counting casualties...

I say, *"I never meant to hurt you"*
and I mean it - but I always meant - to protect myself
I never expected war to my homeland
I bombed first to take control of the invasion
Yet, this terror always planned its attack
From the core of the Big Apple
I traded freedom for the center of this world
Yet, it crumbled eventually

I still hold tribute to who I was meant to be
Hoping one day a broken slave can make amends
With his destiny

I've never been one to be good with intimacy
But I have always been good with my words
I avoided responsibility so eloquently
They way I shift the blame with words through my teeth
Your heart?
I'd dent its walls with my effort to deep clean
Yet my sharp tongue and crooked smile
Forced you to brace it

See, I came from a bloodline of liars
Their heritage written with such promise
His passion - so ocean he would lake her
Yet their sparks just turned to fire

I was forced to repeat this history
Before seed became fertile
From conception, I forced a loose noosed addict
and thin line of naivety to tie their knot
This bow never made for a perfect gift
It strangled hope within their insecurities
Yet I was still born
He - Pro-athlete
She - nurse
When he fumbled as a father she tried her best not to Mis-carry
this birth

I don't remember my first words
But I do remember the pain you would leave me in
When I couldn't utter any

See I never been good with intimacy
but I have always been good with my words
Always...
...until I wasn't.

WHO AM I?

See a smile because I see you
Yet half the things I see through
 like fiberglass and windows
Like beauty without the mental
My doubts are what keeps us into
these bouts I never see the end to
 But then again who am I
my judgments can't be justified
just because of all the things I've sacrificed
to see you excel throughout your life
your potential hails like raining ice
 And falls through your hands because of your own device
you've dropped the ball not once or twice
But who cares if I was there to give you advice
Again I say who am I?
I mean why do I try?
It's your tears I cry
I mean just tell me why
You can't see the light
I mean you can't see what's right
Your worse sense is sight
Your limit is the sky but you're afraid of flight
So you walk in spite
Of a mind so bright
Or your gift to write
Or the times you screamed FLY
But again I say who am I?
I mean who are you
To have a gift that moves

No boundaries or rules

No limits to what you can do

But instead you fail to

Or even attempt to use

You never sharpen your tools

So when it's your time you lose

And all I can do is say I tried to warn you

but again I say who am I

Am I more than the person that stands beside you

The one that you confide to

And I'll open up so you can have a place

That you can hide too

My heart beats inside you

So when you're gonna die too

Have your back like it is mine

So you can say we share a spine too

Can't think but you're on my mind too

Feel lost I'll come and find you

I'll stand and battle when they're clowning

You might as well call this Rize 2

Stuck anywhere I'll be a ride to

You feel enslaved your freedom I'll buy you

Want to get high

I'll ask God to send your angels

Just to show you how to fly too

But again I say who am I?

So now can't you see

That you're important to me

As I sleep with you achieve

Because your goals and my dreams

So unconscious I will be

If you consciously succeed

I'll remain in this coma

But brain dead I won't be

It's your gift from me

To share my mentality

So now now when I ask who am I

I can look in the mirror and say you are me

The father

The thing I lost I have the chance
To mold and nurture with my hands
With love so pure
It will endure
No matter where we land

Yet fear it grips my future hope
Anxiety wins I have no vote
Though I made a shift
Embraced my gifts
There lingers still this foe

So time has come to kill the man
The walking dead alone he stands
For Mirror sees
A father's pleas
To never return to him again

HELLO FEAR

Hello? Yes, 911. I have an emergency!
No, no one is hurt *yet*, but I'm fighting some insecurities And they are torturing
They are kind of relentless
And I don't even sleep cuz they stole my dreams
And the faith that's left inside of me.   I think
they're tryna murder it
Please send help quick!

Have you ever been so desperate that you wish your soul could have emergency surgery?
Like, put me under, then give me open heart to where the chains start
Take a scalpel to my flesh until you cut away all the dead parts

It all started when I was approached with a question the other day
One that made me think
The question was if you could name your greatest fear what would it be?
I pondered for a little bit searched my inner me
Walking through the hallways and corridors to doors locked by only me
Fumbling through my thoughts
Searching for the key
Patting my pockets like that video you seen
Some of you may not get that but all of you have gotten lost trying to find this thing
Wondering, Is it failure or could it be - success or just the enemy?
I read once and seen a film, *Coach Carter,* I believe
You know, you remember that scene when he said, "It's not the darkness, but the light that frightens me?"
But honestly, why does what I fear even have to be a question?
I have battled with excuses for a while now
Hands bloodied, eyes blacked, and knees bowed
Shirt ripped so i can't wear my emotions on my sleeve now

Contempt so tired of running that now i got my feet bound
I quit cuz apparently, I made this into a lifestyle
So sick and tired of being forced to swallow this defeat down
Focus has always been hard for me, with distractions and people
see I'm using an excuse now

See, I have battled excuses for a while now
Toiled with the torment of the dark side
Until I found my inner Jedi
Dear Lord, this enemy is after me trying to Sith my faith And
leave me Anakin
Darth, I mean so dark - you can't defeat this light
Saber you down, prepare to fight. This Force has more!
Have you seeing stars you Know tHis means war!

See, if God has never given us the spirit of fear then Where did it
come from?
Where does your power range from?
Is it defeat or dominion?
We've replaced a sound mind and strength
With a gift from the dark one

He said fly on wings like eagles
Who said your Soardone (Zordon)?
See you never have to stand alone
Heavens sent you safety like an Angel Grove
See this team brings Hope
And If you ever let fear change your mind
The Alpha gives you power
See, it's Morphin Time!
Fear was never meant to be part of your design
I want to divorce my fear until I'm no longer that 'X' man
Even in midst of the Storm ill make my last stand
And if I ever go Rogue and ignore God's plan
I hope to See Real Bros (serebro) come and find me again
Night crawl, if I must - if I'm running I can't
So set apart from this Gray it's in my Jean don't you see I'm
mutant

I want to Marvel in His love because there fear won't live

When our faith meets God nothings Impossible you'll read that where Luke is

God as Head Coach is undefeated versus Fear like Saban nick

And the next time someone asks me my greatest fears, I'llll say they don't exist...

DEFINITION OF ME

This is more than just a poem

This is scribe to the history books of my life story

This is author's autograph to stained skin

This is Hieroglyphic tattooed to the stone walls of my existence

This is the playback of dyslexic memories where I've reversed past *my past* just to find my present

I am master astrologer that bled these constellations onto the canvas of this galaxy

Exploding in greatness - call me *Supernova*

So watch this Star War for his force to awaken

Blindside to the old guy just to worship the Christ

Check this Saint Claire Lee (clearly) reference

As I crucify my dark side with this saber pen as I repent

So pardon my Yoda speak

But Definition of me this is

I am poet drowned in a water of Unforgiveness

Where pardon sins still smother me

Daring me to breathe

I had become a slave man to my failures

Dragging around a dead man

Until I brought this Django to where these chains go!

And this change - gone come in...

Since Sam made it clear it's been a long time coming

I no longer run from my past

It makes me beautiful...

I am the southern sun-kissed melanin

Warmed over by summers in California

Bred to make an impact

I have the heartbeat of a giant

Chasing a heart like David

Seeking redemption daily

Growing up in a generation where they swore our skin color no longer matters

But everything matters...

I can't get my hands up quick enough

But I won't be defined by a massacred upbringing that has cursed generations to believe that because you look different you are somehow better than me

I am compassion - married to hope - running through the veins of this outstretched arm

Pulling others into their dreams

Don't believe?

Roll up my sleeve

Insert IV

Doctor check and see

Repeat yoda speak

Definition of me this is...

I am a father to a little girl who will never have to search for love in the back seats of manipulation

Who won't fall into the arms of disaster searching for a void that he took responsibility for - that he never had the strength to fill in any way

She will know real men exist

and they look 6 foot 3"

Slightly athletic... *ok maybe chubby...*

But still the most handsome man in her eyes.

Best kiss to her cheek

Chocolate-coated pigment - with the bellows of ancestors, explode when he speaks - to touch the tips of her ears and dreams as she sleeps

As she visualizes God's Love and her own destiny

Allowing soft whispers from her lips to leave - repeating over and over -

This is the definition of me.

I am royalty; better yet - I am king!

Made in the image of a father who loved me despite my sin - who knew me before my own mother did...

Handcrafted, manufactured, signed, sealed, and delivered! Stamped with approval...

Heaven's Kid!

Bathed in a 2000-year-old water that bled out from a crucifix...

Given a tongue that strokes a canvas into an oil masterpiece...

Yet, sharp like a sword on both its ends

Bred to be a warrior and my armor is darker-skinned

Shield my faith so you can't defeat (da feet) this peace or waste (waist) this truth...

And right to his (righteous) chest, you know,

Straight to the heart of men - connected to the source... it's so supernatural it seems fantasy like it's Wakandan

Since the enemy wants war then we're dropping bombs in

It is challenge day and we have watched from the mountains, then came down to let the fight begin!

And shhh - here's the secret...

I've been already guaranteed a win!

So before this ends,

I want to remind you once again

That in Him - I'm complete!

Forget Yoda Speak...

This is the definition of me.

WHEN THUNDER SPEAKS

I have looked beyond the dark moon skies

Overwhelmed by the warmth of its whispers

I sought out decisions in the glistens of the fog lights

Hoping passion could marry destiny in its dusks

I am mere mortal to the mighty puppeteer

Strings of fear have long laced my limbs

I have searched for answers in an ocean of Unforgiveness

Drowning in what resembled redemption

Only to have the taste of destruction on my breath

Gulps of dissatisfaction plagued my insides

There is moral to this story

I am mixed emotions made mural

This culture's my canvas

Paint brush strokes of midnight

Until again I play artist to moonlight

Rays dance on the face of water's bodies like classic keys

Playing Masterpiece where creativity sprouts out of the box like Jack and it hits the road indeed

This is where whispering dreams meet the roar in me

Silenced by a timidity that played muzzle to marching orders

Muddied these massive waters where the precipitation made its home

See the skies cried when I ignored its boom and failed to Go

Fear made a righteous path into quick-sanded memories

Every declaration became just wasted energy

Every prophetic seed sown relentlessly was retracted by your local enemy

But there's something that's still burning within my inner me

I made theme song to the sound of oratorical Conversation had at mountains peak

Played at the rhythm at which purpose beats

Brightened by the sequence in the sky at the space where earth and lightning meets

This is the opposite of blasphemy birthed from a holy incubator mother womb so majestic -   It was destined to be named *legacy*

The blueprint to creating all you see came from the parting lips of eternity

Left through the true ghost of Christmas past   The only King who was the perfect

Sacrifice to rip the veil and bleed to walk on this earth Until 33 and live blemish

Free wrapped in just as much flesh as you and me

Do you hear the sky as it roars instructions through flickered imagery?

Like Habakkuk 2:2-3

Take Palm to recycled trees to allow pen to bleed

And make it clear enough for men to see

What the end looks like from infancy

This is a culture shock and awakening

Antidotes and vaccines to the plagued and poisoned sheep

This is a supernatural disaster to all impurities

This is flash floods of adolescents into maturity

This is where the faults are shifted and erected idols become ruined streets

This is massive whirlwind to your plain and rural peace

This is spark to the wildfire of your dried and fallen leaves of dreams

This is what happens *When Thunder Speaks...*

I AM A BIG BABY

They laugh at me because I am always crying
They say I am a big baby
They say men don't cry like that
They, they never ask where my tears come from...

They never investigate the gate that once kept
These tears damned
They never offer tissue to wipe away tears toxic from Tumultuous
trauma's tactical torture
They never understand how long it took me to dig Into the wells
of my emotions
They never acknowledge the healed man that stands Before them
They never knew I was an assassin
To flesh and hearts
They don't know I massacred many innocent women Through my
insecurities
Penetrated their soul and took them hostage

They, women, even played a part in my captivity
They enslaved my emotions by mocking my manhood, berated
my sensitivity
They'd scold when I cried
And then cried when I was cold
They complained about my emotions
Then complained when they were gone
They couldn't see how big I loved until I gave them Broken hearts
They don't understand how hard it was to arrest that Fugitive and
my tears were my reward

They assumed I had hard times
They never asked me why, i never had to serve it
They never honor my acquittal or my redemption That pours
down my cheeks in droplets
They never offer shoulders, only sulfuric snickers
They burn at the bridge that I have securely Equipped to do what
they've asked,
"Get over it!"

They rather me look violent than look victim
They don't realize these tears are trophies from pain I took first place in
They don't hear the victory in my whaling
They, culture, prefer Carbon copied Cons instead of Crying creatives
They try to castrate my masculinity then expect me Not to emote from the injury
Oh what irony!

They prefer labels like *wimpy* or *sissy*
They don't see the compliment because it takes Strength to stand under a title that may isolate you from Society
Like *Christian* - Or *black*
They swear they don't see color but my tears are Murals painted on my cheeks
They have seen tears like these before
They recognize the scars yet they refuse to take responsibility for being the one who created them

They marred my history
Beat the dough out of me
Then obligated me to fit within
This cookie cutter identity

They rather hear me roar, than weep
Yet, they muzzle the beast attempt to force me to do circus feets
They call me primate but even monkeys squall when The lion king's deceased
They ignore my rain like tears
But it still won't make my Pride Rock
They can't see that these tears are my emancipation
So I'll cry road maps just so other little black boys Can avoid death traps

My tears are the Sojournered Truth to America the Honestless
I rather my eyes be empty
Than that dream you promised us!
I hold these truths to be self-evident

That all tears are created equal
That each drop is my John Hancock to the fire
 of an independence that they tried to smolder

They aren't entitled to choking up my tear ducts
Not matter how much their privilege my suffocate us
I'll cry relentlessly

Go ahead and laugh
At every part of me
And I'll be the big baby
Because my tears are a sign
I can finally breathe

THE OUTKAST

I'm sorry, Ms Jackson!
WOOOO - I am for real.
Never meant to make your daughter cry.
I apologize a trillion times.

I'm sorry, Ms Jackson!
WOOOO - I am for real.
Never meant to make your daughter cry.
I apologize a trillion times.

I had to make amends
with Miss Jackson, Miss Williams, *and* Miss Davis
for how I treated their kids.

I was a "PLAYER"
and that ANTHEM resonated
through everything that I did

It was innate
While THE WHOLE WORLD learned how to love
I learned love through their hate

I remember feeling OUTKAST to my own home
They said, *"Be a BIG BOY"*
I felt more like a squirrel chasing nuts beyond Drey
3000 miles from anywhere I belonged

All I wanted was a hug
I offered my affection as ROSES
But they would just PARK it in the seat next to them
The rejection felt like BOMBS on B.

My LOVE left BELOW
That pain would BOX this SPEAKER
Leaving me silent
My voice awaiting its LIBERATION

This caused a trickle-down effect
Where my only image of passion
Came through sex or remorse

Where a "HAPPY VALENTINES DAY"
could end in something like
a HOLLYWOOD DIVORCE

I was taught to take the perfect woman's fairytale
and pour GASOLINE on her DREAMS
I was the PROTOTYPE prince charming it seemed
then eventually it was the RETURN OF THE G

This became my norm.
My everyday routine.
Start my morning off SO FRESH
My heart, SO CLEAN

Ending with a trap set so well
And was dug so deep
I convinced you it was a privilege
To fall in with me

THE ART OF STORYTELLING
Was something I mastered
Combined deception with partial truths
A mixed drink of emotions
Intoxicated by THE WAY YOU MOVE

I encouraged the affection
Explained that I CAN'T WAIT
Repeated the regimen on multiple dates
I took my own collection
In the offering plate

I was so cold
My core obtuse
I lied to ME AND YOU
YO MAMMA AND YO COUSIN TOO
Leaving us so low
That even an ELEVATOR
couldn't reach this floor

I became tired
Overwhelmed with shame
This PLAYER'S BALL was popped
and my name defamed

I was lonely
Done staring at this hollow shell of a man
Enduring a poisonous pain
Brought on by my own hands

I whispered gently to the broken child
a HUMBLE MUMBLE
It's time for you to GIT UP and GIT OUT

To wake up and be proud
To stare into every mirror
Exclaiming HEY YA
But first - I had to make amends
With many mothers
For many lies, during many nights

I'm sorry Ms Jackson!
WOOOO- I am for real.
Never meant to make your daughter cry.
I apologize a trillion times.

ODE TO MY HEIRESS

I have been birthed a responsibility that I never thought I'd be
ready for
So worried that these hands,
calloused from clawing out of my own despair
would scar you - carrying you away from yours
Hands like magnets
bold enough to make my palms meet
hoping these prayers can prevent preyers and still leave space to
rock you to sleep
Fearful that this battered man wouldn't be delicate enough to
care for his first flower
Dandelion to this rain storm
Angst, whirlwind my emotions
Blinding the eye of this tornado
Trembling, are my crane arms
Folding under pressure
Origami to the weight your life carries
Yet still honored at the fact that heaven chose this troubled
Tennesseean to be
Titan after your destiny

You are like a diamond in the rough
No, you're like the toy at the bottom
of the Cracker Jack box
No, you are like oxygen because even if I take you for granted - I
can't live without you
I've taken you for granted and not honored the moments I get to
breathe
You're more than just a seed
You are like a butterfly that flaps its wings
into rainbows that lead
to pots of gold in homes where unicorns roam
You are the Abracadabra to my greatest trick
and *tricks are for kids*
so I'll pull a rabbit out of every hat I can
just to make sure everything you deserve
you can get
Like your mother does and my mother did.

You are like sunshine after days of rain
You are the reason I know heaven exists
You are elegance with a warriors heartbeat
You are a dream worth fighting for
and I'll be the first in the ring

I want to *Brown vs Board* the two halves of every one of your
separately (but equal) broken hearts
I'll volunteer as tribute so your love never catches fire, nor never
loses its hunger due to his games
I'll be doctor to your pain
until your first love turns to, *what's his name?*

I may never get his name right
I just hope I never have to remind him of mine
I want to play *patty cake* until my fingers hurt
I wanna hurt every demon you point your finger towards
I will tell you not to be afraid of the dark
I will send angels to make their mark
on every dream turned nightmare
I want to beat up your nightmares and every shadow that comes
out your closet
I won't be perfect, but in all purpose, I'll magic erase every
mistake you'll make
I will be your tissue when you are sick
I will resuscitate your faith when you're flatlined and hopeless
I'll be bridge over the moat to your insecurities
He's already sent a King who has sacrificed for your life
So I only have to be knight for every dragon that attempts to keep
you dungeoned
I want to be your first Prince Charming
First date
First dance
First hand
given to the last man you will spend your life with
I want to spend my life loving you
because love covers a multitude
and this inheritance is the greatest gift
my heiress can look forward to

LAST FLIGHT

Our Father, which art in heaven
Hallowed be thy name
Thy kingdom come
Thy will be done...
But sometimes,
Thy will taste a little like heartbreak -
Feel a bit like abandonment

I come before the heavy burdened
Knowing the weight is great enough
for the father to bear
But I choose to bear it anyway
I choose to hold onto everlasting memories Drenched in the
excitement I had in your presence

Elegant.
I call you that to honor the woman you were...

Not many could wear the shade of life you did on your skin - and
still smile
Not many could lose sleep over the thought of others' pain -
and still find the strength to fight through theirs

Survivor.
I call you that because you carried resilience
In the tone of your voice
Passion that resounded past frozen stone walls
that encased our hearts
You are the subtle irony in creation
Perfection molded into fractured masterpiece
With a few hidden secrets

We could only keep you temporarily
Your hands were weakened
Only because you consistently kept them outstretched for others
to grab onto

Rain, sleet, snow, cold, or flu
You always made yourself available
Have you ever seen a bird with a clipped wing?
You would sacrifice your feathers
Peacock just so others would dare to be beautiful When they fly

Gorgeous.
You were gorgeous
Carried excellence in your glide
Patience in your eyes
Your lips were full with affirmation
You strived to place mirrors in front of every child so They could never forget who they were
We will never forget *who you are...*

Legacy.
It was left in the wind
We take deep breaths of your memory
Clouds park themselves on melancholy cheeks
In skies that still drop reminders of you
We stored you deep in our hearts
Hoping your passion could be extracted by our roots
Leaving your mark on our limbs

Even when you leave
There's still space
for the caterpillar in me to find safety
Even though death tried to force cocoon your Beauty
And bury your life
But her fly
Your name shall be etched into the chest of lost Children in a language they can only recognize
As their own
It will tell them that life is short
but their purpose isn't
It will remind them it's not what you have
but why you have it

Hero.
The name I'll remember you most as
One who died in the battlefield

with a sword in one hand

and truth in the other...

MIRROR MIRROR

Mirror mirror on the wall

Can you change this reflection to anyone else at all

Can you take away these sleepless nights

Where fairytales have traded places

With nightmares

Where tears have become regular resident to my bedside

Where loneliness has enslaved me to her torture

I fell to her will around the time I lost my own

Mirror you promised me my image would reflect His

Yet this sub par picture doesn't even come close

I have memories of past pains that still stain All I put my hands too

I'm a. Made made from mistakes made of mistakes afraid to make a mistake

I lay awake playing mental patty cake with the thoughts of my shortcomings

Like you want me to free my people and part the sea

But can't you see I'm still still still stuttering

And you said on this rock you could build but instead of skipping water I'm just submerging

and even with your outstretched hand this fragmented man falls through the cracks of your fingers like fragmented sand

It's clear from Joshua's life you always had a plan

But I wonder if I wandered to far off from this promised land

Mirror I have circled this life more than seven times in search of truth yet still I only worship you lion king

I can still hear my fathers screams

You deliberately disobey me

You refused to change a thing

It cut me deep so

I ran away just so i wouldn't

Have to see this Scar again

Mirror I am tired of seeing the same images

I had to run to the jungle to finally find my pardon sins

From my father

I could no longer move slow I murals

I can still hear the voice of my guardians

Deep raw whispering

Looook harder

I knew everything I thought was true was laced in faltered realities

No longer must I suffer my self imposed exile

There's a land awaiting it's king's return

I was born an heir to majesty

When life left just enough rope to bear noose I broke loose

Mirror you finally gave me a vision worth glancing

My hands couldn't scribe these words quick enough

Blood drenched tablets told stories of unrelenting love

That played lullabies to my hearts forgiveness

Freedom tasted like a quenching of a lifetimes of thirst

Baron dreams resurrected by the waters of the nile

Fighting with denial

resuscitating destiny that seemed deceased for a while

My Father dug farther to foster where I faltered

He reignited my light until my image was altered

Mirror it was never your job to give me identity in the first place

Reflections finally conceived who i was meant to be

royalty

beautiful

His masterpiece

Autographed by my designer

Signed in blood

sealed in resurrection

and affirmed in his spirit

Just so I can stare into the heart of any mirror

and reflect HIS IMAGE

AIN'T I AMERICAN

Days like this
Make you refuse to take
Every inhale for granted

MAKES YOU FEEL:
That breathing is a privilege not a right
That existing is optional
If you have triggered fearful
Whites or blues
It's crazy these are the main two colors of the American flag...our
blood makes the third
We have saturated this soil for centuries
Birthed their riches without recompense
Like our asks have been absurd

I run from the thought in my head
Where I have been weaponized by birth
Like human right was to make victim white
If there happens to be a black man in sight

I cry because it's the only emotion
That shows vulnerability
Maybe that can keep me safe
Maybe my tears will serve
As a shield to those
Who've targeted me with their hate
Maybe my pain could...
No it's just another reason
To express their own

For generations we have John Henried
Our railroad
Praying it take us somewhere
Before our hearts gave out
Endurance built less than civil
War won on our backs

Like the scars that you have engraved
Our history with
Backs against the wall
You think we won't fight back
Where wings have clashed and clapped
Each time you created another black angel

Sip from the cup of what you've brewed
Be this no Boston tea
Yet our party STILL political
See we've rioted and looted
Uprooted you from your everyday routine
The true American way

Ain't I American?

Yet we don't hold these truths to be self evident because you lied
for far too long

We don't wait for you to endow us
With certain rights because
It's clear we alien to your human

We don't dare ask for equality
We know it's all the same race
Until we start winning
Until we have built our own refuge
From wooden scraps

You will bring out the Tulsa Torches
You will Birmingham Bomb our Beatitudes
Turn blessings to ash
Insurrection to the institution
Of our independence
Declaring your own chokehold
Our chosen
Kneel on the neck of our needs
Cry wolf when we have been mere sheep

So we will lion roar until our whole pride comes
Until our pride runs deep and seeps into white Sheets you have kept hung
Blood sweat
And we know you've had some
Deep breathes like it's your last one
And let's see who it is you'll call on
Face pink watch it turn to blue cheek
Now I see how my skin was too dark to be seen as American

ON THE OTHER SIDE

I believe I have cried more in the last month than the last year

I have drained gutters filled with an unrelenting rainstorm of tears

I have tried to pacify my own pain with melodic memories

Attempted to finger-paint Joy back into my daydreams
Oil pastel brushstrokes of hope into my lonesome gazes

I have carved holographic grins into my cheeks that short circuit too often
Glitches to remind me the pains still here
Static memories tells me to box my vision
Blurs the image
Repair the feed until i see clear
But i still freeze from fear

laid in the lap of loss and lingered
Wondered if this hollowed out skeletal cell
Could ever hold my heart again or has it become too dungeon too dingy
too slavery to my postpartum from premature delivery
evacuated expectations my purpose seemed
To incubated to be released to me

The truth is Loss this time felt like a knockout blow like i wouldn't last another round
I looked around waiting for someone to throw in the towel
Waiting for some one to wave the white flag
Yet white seemed to pure to pull on my behalf

And voice in my head kept screaming stay down stay down
Paralyzed i remained on the ground
This time

I thought i was gonna drown
This time I though
that i have have finally went too deep,
chained to boulders of emotions
sin that made me sink
Linked to every mistake
my mind never skipped a beat
Bottom never came so fast
Never felt so thick
Doormat read welcome home
Key a perfect fit
Failure swung the door wide open
Shame said come in and sit
Guilt had made my bed
And Insecurities dared me to lie in it

Lost at sea was an understatement
My displacement had me facing violent truths that crashed like
waves did
Unable to evade it
Yet failure wasn't my end
To my own amazement
I might have hit rock bottom
But I never embraced it

I refuse to suffocate from my own suffering
I refuse to relent
I refuse to abandon boat when the ship begins to sink i
remembered i could swim
I refuse to recluse into abandon caverns
And hide my secrets in
I had to find the bottom to plant my feet and push back off again

Air never came so fast
Never gasped so deep
When death and disease attacks our lung
I recall who first showed us how to breathe
Inhale purpose exhale tragedy
Inhale forgiveness HIS excellence and majesty

Exhausted and tired i succumbed and sank to my enemies
Then He walked on water towards me and told me keep that
same energy
See i know pain defeat disaster and
Destruction
Depression and detours shame to self Sabotage internal
corruption
No matter how dark and dim it may get in the night
Morning always comes and he welcomes you first with light

On the other side

I IMAGINE

I imagine angels met you at the gates with a standing ovation

I imagine the well done's acknowledging your faithful service
came shortly after.

I imagine you causing uproars of laughter

I imagine heaven is exactly how you pictured
Perfect like every scripture
You read at the head of the dining room table
Daily
3:00PM
I imagine daily you still sitting there reading words of life that you
would soon actualize

I imagine sometimes that your still alive
A selfish desire

I imagine you finally resting
I imagine stories being told for generations of the hero you were
Superman to a Compton clan

And your Louis lane had a sultry voice
And this Louis name was Joyce

Victory came in your ability to conquer poverty
To conquer curses that wiped out black families generationally

I imagine that you had a conversation with God like Deuteronomy
33
Blessing and protecting every part of your legacy

I imagine days before your last breathe
On your last leg
You took heed to Jesus in Gethsemane
Where in Matthew 26:41 he said

To Watch and pray
And i am sure you did because your spirit was always strong even
as your body withered away

I imagine that you Miss Your Baby and family
Yet heaven had an assigned seat for you and you always showed
up on time

See there always is a time
A time to weep and a time to laugh,
A time to mourn and a time to dance
I imagine that we will be spending time doing it all

I Imagine how strong you had to be just to hold on. To carry
yourself from sickbed to walker
You were a soldier by the definition
You embodied LOVE AND FAMILY IN EVERYTHING YOU DID

I was there for your last breathe
I watched it leave your lips
I still remember the sound
Holy Spirit told me it would happen
So I was prepared for this
And no one else was around
I Imagine your last breathe matched your first in heaven
That last exhale would accel you to excel into his excellence
I Imagine that when the world is struggling as a whole to breathe
that you decided to selflessly
Be one less person taking up oxygen
That you went home to get it settled in for us.
That you pioneered past roads the world tried to lay out for you
I imagine that you have sown prayers that only Synai may
manifest
That the earth quaked when the weight you carried shifted

I imagine you are preparing to drop your mantle
That we are your greatest treasure
That we will carry your name into spaces you never even Imagined
I Imagine that we will be in position when this all happens

In position to watch you be carried up
To Catch legacy you left
You didn't leave us
You are just continuing to lead the way
My prayer is that we make you proud in your absence
And into eternity
Because I imagine that we will be there together

FOR YEARS

For years
I have had to battle many ugly truths
One being that though your memories may be the Vehicle you are given
It doesn't have to be the one driving too
Your history is the currency for fees left
by a generational noose
Dead things are only meant to be revived if they're all Made new
And for a long time I wrestled with who had their Hands at 10 & 2

Yet one thing I knew
I am the little boy
Who could no longer hide in the shadows of his past
Whose fears could no longer cascade melancholy Clouds over
where his tombstones housed
Who could no longer be victim to the villain that Maliciously
muzzled his mouth
And since the one from Nazareth
Called up Lazarus
We can all behold the new man now
Though his shame brought the pain
It ran down his cheek
From his bloodshot window panes
Transfused truth and brought life to lies
That ran through his veins
Knock three times and call out his name
And watch the reveal of a wildling tamed
Yet cycles same
They call insane

For years
I have heavied this heartache
Dragged boulders of brokenness
Burdened bricks of a barren boyhoods
Battered bodies and bruised beauty
Buried young Brandon's left

Unbrazened and branded
It felt like abandoned prayers and days mishandled

It looked like lost boys in a land where Pan was never Man enough
to return
Children seeking a lord who still flies
Whose voice needs no conch shell to be heard
Children who lost the miracle in the magic
Made them mere muggles
Muddied memories in moats where mistakes merged
Children born too demi to face mountains so Olympic
Where thundered threats progress
To their lightning surge
What happens when we are no longer concerned

When burnout numbs the nerves to our hearts
Brings atrophy to our empathy
Paralysis to our patience and persistency
Simbas ran recklessly
From where they were called to king
Who is left to be scarred

When we no longer
Enter classrooms to coach and coax
The ails of angered adolescents
Endangered from untreated aggression
Address the their angst
And empty eyes that can't focus on lessons
Mend marred motivation through captivating Conversations that
frees captive creatives
Create spaces for transformable healing
Instead of simply chasing stages
Stage interruptions to intervene their sabotage
Derail their trains set on the path of wreckage
Wreck plans set to destroy their world
Avenge those promised their end
What game could finally win this endless war

See I was told that heroes need fewer capes
and more hope
More hands to hold more close
More clothes to clothe more souls
More songs to sing more free
Fewer fees for more tolls
More told stories of those who love more
And fewer loathe

It's time to see what happens
When we unleash more ropes

What happens when voices
Meet ears like antidotes
To the plagues of past trauma
When voices whose vulnerable volume
Lay groundwork to new emotions
When voices solicit safe haven nd social refuge
When voices liberate those labored in old behaviors
What happens when voices disembark those Anchored to
poisonous ports
When voices teach students to plot a new course

We must decide what matters more
We must take time to heal so they aren't left ignored
We must create rhythms that keep a consistent pour
We must remember
That we aren't the heroes
They are waiting for
We must show them
Inside lies all they need to explore
We must be vessels to the victories
They have in store

And one day maybe
They will tell tales
Of how they swam to the shores
Of hope through an ocean of tears
And finally lived out their healing
For years

LOVE LIKE

Have u ever had real love

Not that Valentine tv glitz glammed and shine love

That on time love

That linger lasting on your mind love

That hard to find love

That masterfully crafted by design love

That finally it's arrived love

That first dawn sunshine love

That masterpiece across the sky love

That seek no matter where you hide love

That peace when life goes awry love

That put it all on the line love

That willingness to fight love

That when your blind I'll give you sight love

That consistent sacrifice love

That in the darkness be your light love

That drawn in and hypnotize love

That reminds you that you're alive love

That stares you deep within your eyes love

That boldness when you're shy love

That truth to where you lie love

That no in between it's black or white love

That have your back like it is mine love

That you can say we share a spine

That rescue type love

The send your son to die love

That comfort when you cry love

That lashing on your back lacerations with the glass for refusing to deny love

That last breath leaving lips with head lifted high Love

That see it's this no limits love

That it is finished love

That can't be diminished love

That keeps me repented love

That changes my vision love

That knew the end from the beginning love

That never stays offended love

That makes broken things mend in love

That solely dependent love

That never stays hindered love

That guarantees Im winning love

That grace and forgiving love

That everlasting healing love

That past has been cleared in love

So that one day you live in neverending love

CARTOONS & CHAOS

As a kid I remember Saturday mornings
Were filled with
Breakfast
Yardwork
And of course cartoons
Sweat from my brow wiped away
As animated joy would fill our room
Refilled what was poured out that day
Refreshed as we watched the next
Episode after episode
It was like lived on repeat
A place of escape
Because reality always seemed
To get the best of me
It was as if my childhood was themed
To the reruns
I have cried on so many floors
That the carpet could scream
Testimonies of my chaos
No hiding
You couldn't *Duck Tales*
Just listen
I bet that *Rugrats*
Allow me to play an episode
And let the *Talespin*
As a child I never seemed to fit in
Whether home or in the classroom
Only on courts and in fields
Is where I found safety

There I could be *LEGEND*
And those *HIDDEN TEMPLES*
Could protect me
School time would make me playground patsy
Educators would ignore my whaling like bad acting
Even *RECESS* would remind me of my race like its a Track meet
Remind me of this *Wild Thorn* buried in my side
No matter how deep I *Doug* funny thing is
I still couldn't remove the sting of this RERUN

These are more than memories
These were engrained
Into childhood as normalcy

I stood out like a sore thumb
an outcast
As a teenager I felt more mutant than human being
Wishing I could hide like a ninja
Duck into my turtle shell
Yet I just always failed
New season
SAME HELL
New channel
Same tale
Cold rain
Pain hails

New tears
Same cry
Same *Blues*, no *Clues* why
Lonely *Sailor Moon* high
When Ship sunk took new Ride

Rocket Power to Blue Skies

My voice *Tiny* yet *Toons* the tide

When booms the thunder that changes lives

Me in control of my world,

I could no longer stand it

Until I surrendered

To the real *Captain* of this *Planet*

Then my story changed and the channel too

So when the credits roll, His Glory's due.

Acknowledgments

I want to take the time to first acknowledge my Lord and Savior Jesus Christ. Without Him my life would be lost and broken and empty. I also want to thank my parents Edward and Carolyn Allen for every sacrifice you have ever made to see me become my best. I also want to thank my Spiritual Parents Sherman and Jaquet Dumas, who took on the task to help continue to shape me and help reshape parts of my destiny into one that will leave a legacy. I want to acknowledge my brother Matthew for looking at me and always seeing my best even when the most rotten parts showed. I want to thank Brittany Watkins for being an amazing mother and allowing me to grow as the father to our daughter. I want to thank Synai Joy Allen for allowing me to father her and being the best thing to ever come into my life. I would like to acknowledge my family for always having my back, my friends for standing with me and investing in me. This is the beginning of something amazing. For anyone who I missed or didn't acknowledge please forgive me.

About the Author

Poet, motivational speaker, artist, minister, father, Christ-follower. These descriptive words embody Brandon Christopher Allen. Born on January 23, 1987, to a loving mother and father, then later a younger brother. Brandon was raised in Memphis, TN and learned fast how societal norms affected his self esteem and relationships.

The effect of addiction and struggles that stem from it, played part into what led to many poor decisions, pride, and continued failures, that eventually ended with homelessness. Feeling muted and discarded he slipped into a dark destitute state. Holding on by a thread he searched for an answer to the hovering question: "why don't I just give up?" Then in 2009 he had an encounter almost like an awakening. He had an experience with God that was more alive than he could ever imagine and it pushed him into seeking a relationship he never truly had. From a Father he never really knew. This opened the door into his destiny.

In Brandon's poetic work and profound thoughts about life events and his walk with Christ, you learn exactly what happens "WHEN THUNDER SPEAKS" by gaining insight into a world that is equally balanced with the ugly truth and the beauty of coming out on the other side. His passion for community, Christ, and building up those who come in contact with him are only a few of his gifts.

As the Program Director of Rescue A Generation, founded by Rodriguez, Brandon pushes to motivate a generation through life changing engagement. The vision and fruition of his creative mind can be seen in the works of his clothing line PA APPAREL, SPOKEN WORD, and LIFE's MISSION of being a voice for those who can't speak for themselves.

Proverbs 31:8
Speak up for those who cannot speak for themselves;
ensure justice for those being crushed.